Me, unapologetically.

Kimberley Labbon

BookLeaf Publishing

Presentation by *BookLeaf Publishing*

Web: www.bookleafpub.com

E-mail: info@bookleafpub.com

ISBN: 9789358318791

First edition 2023

Dedicated to you.

There won't be another you

Do you realise how much had to be done, to make sure you existed? Gravity had to pull matter from the edges of space to create millions of stars and galaxies..

Stars had to explode
Particles had to collide
Planets had to form
Oceans had to be filled
Forests had to grow
Humans had to evolve
Cities had to be built
Lives had to be lived
Choices had to be made

And even if time is infinite, There will never be another you.

I am

I am
happy but sad
Present but lost
Satisfied but yearning
Fulfilled but overwhelmed
Confident but insecure
Disappointed but glad
Patient but proud
Open but shut

Unconditional Love

You taught me what unconditional love means;

It means loving me through all my mood swings,

It means loving me through all my weight changes

It means loving me when I'm too sick to look my best

It means loving me when I'm too busy to give you attention

It means loving me on the days I don't want to get out of bed

It means loving me even when I say I don't love you

It means loving me even when I don't love myself

You love me through all stages of life and all forms of my spirit.

3 AM Thoughts

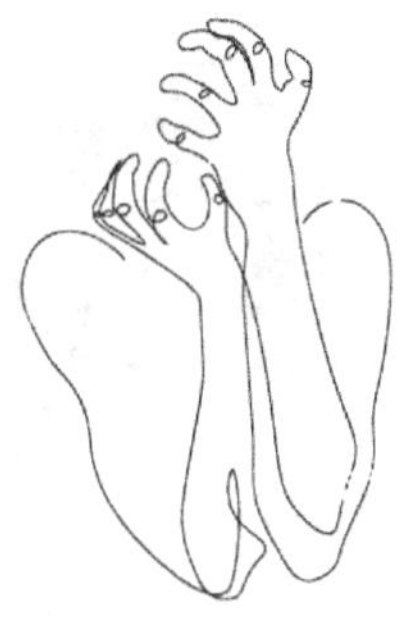

Here I am,
Barely awake,
Barely asleep
Just existing,
Because I have to
Because I need to
Because I care
Because people care
Because I daydream of better things
Because it's human instinct to keep gulping air
But here I am
Barely awake
Barely asleep.

This is my heart, this is my soul, this is my
mind, this is me…

Time..

Let time flow through you
Time isn't something you can grasp in your
hands like an object, it's not something you can
make, merely delegate.

It can't be measured by the number of
accomplishments or failures in life. It's
something you experience in every single breath
you take

It's something that moves through the stars till
they implode, moves through planets till they
explode and moves through matter, like nothing
does.

It exists to remind you that even though you
can't hold it,
Even though you can't make more of it,
It lives within you.
It's yours. It's mine. It's ours.

A different kind of grief

I'm not grieving you,
I'm grieving the idea of you. The idea of you
embracing me after a bad day. The idea of you
simply smiling at me because you're happy to
see me.

The idea of you saying you love me, maybe not
every day but at least enough to make me feel it.
The idea of being just like the hallmark movies
you love so much. I'm grieving the idea of what
you could of meant to me.

I'm grieving a relationship we never had. I'm
grieving the support you never gave me. I'm
grieving all the times you never said you were
proud of me.

I'm grieving the fact that I will never grieve you,
just the idea of you.. and sometimes that'll make
me sad but that's okay, because I'll make sure I'm
never grieved merely by the idea of who I
should of been.

She reads energy

She reads energy,
You can save your words,
She understands you through,
your body language,
your tone of voice,
your eye contact
and your presence.

The spiral

All it takes is one thought...
Just one..
I feel like I spoke too much last night..
Maybe I'm being annoying..
Why am I so annoying?
I should just stop talking..
Why can't I just stop talking?
I'm so weird..
Why am I so weird?
I hate the way I am..
I should just be quiet..
I feel so awkward now..
I'm tired..
Maybe I should lie down for a while..
Maybe I should just stay in bed..
I can't move..
I can't get out of bed..
Not again..

Crossroads

The path you choose to take might start to look narrower and the lights might look like they are dimming; Just take your time, it will all make sense as you go. Before you know it, you'll see the light at the end of the tunnel.

For the believers

Waves crash against the rocks but the shore never waivers. Success is for the believers and risk-takers.

I Miss You

It's okay to miss something you never had but...

The idea of something you always wanted can
take over your whole perception of reality
You can't hold onto it, because that path you
never took, led you to a path you needed to take
The future you had in your head, won't take into
account life's twists and turns.
The parts you think need filling, are rooms of
yourself that can be filled with more of you.

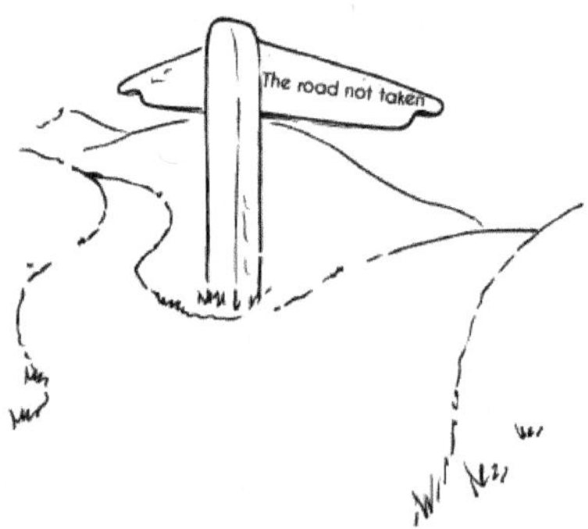

All of you stop talking.

The idea of letting you go, is less than appealing to the voices in my head.

Buckle up

Life's a rollercoaster, but I'll help buckle you in and hold your hand because you're not going anywhere. We're riding this shit storm out together.

Present

The greatest gift you'll ever receive is the
present, because it's here, now and alive

To My Best Friend

She loves with all her heart, and doesn't ask for it in return.

She has seen me at my worst, and offered nothing but support.

She has seen me at my best, and cheered louder than everyone in the crowd.

Forget soul mates, I found my soul sister.
She embodies resilience in a confident manner.

She is..
..Beautiful
..Bold
..Fierce
..Caring
..Kind
..Protective
..Irreplaceable

Just Breathe

Just breathe darling,

Inflate your lungs with possibilities, just as a hot air balloon pilot inflates a balloon in order to take flight to better heights. Inhale all the wonder and curiosity that this lifetime has to offer.

Hold it.

Exhale..
Exhale all the immense doubt, taking up space in your lungs. Exhale the fear that you'll be overwhelmed by life's challenges and make room for triumphs.

Sometimes

Sometimes I feel like my skin aches,

Sometimes I hear my self-doubt louder than my laugh,

Sometimes I wake up and my first emotion is disappointment.

Sometimes I look out the window and see no escape.

Sometimes I hear 'I Love You' and it makes me nauseous.

Sometimes I relax into my awful thoughts.

Sometimes I scream in my sleep and wake up
still screaming in my head.

Sometimes I feel empty.

Sometimes I feel useless.

Sometimes I feel pointless.

Sometimes I feel alone.

Sometimes I feel lost...

...But only sometimes.

A little note to say

...Don't change who you are, people like you
never go out of style...

Black Sheep

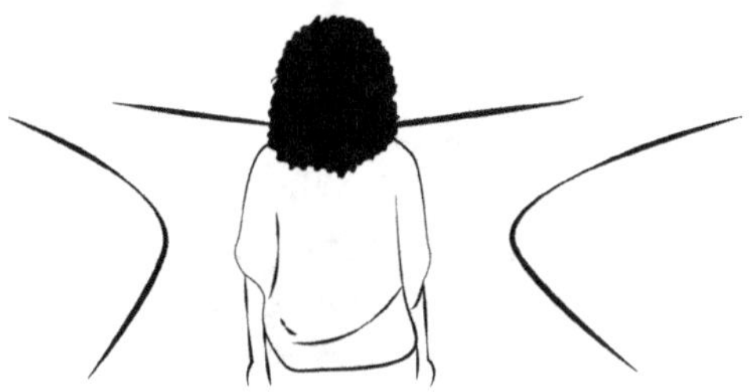

What does being the black sheep even mean?

Someone who doesn't have the same characteristics as their siblings?

Someone who doesn't have the same beliefs as their family?

Someone who goes against the grain?

Someone who gets told their head's in the clouds?

Someone who feels like an outcast?

...Maybe, but I think it means someone who is uniquely beautiful.

Happy Thoughts

Today's a good day, you're in a good head space.
You'll get everything you want and need. All
you have to do is nurture that thoughtful seed.
The seed that's been in the back of your mind.
An idea of something better, greater, happier.

Let your passion be the reason to get up every
day. You've come so far, look how much you've
grown. You'll be unstoppable my dear.

And just like the sunflower you are, you'll rise
higher than even you expected.
Your presence alone, can have the power to
mold a future, where you'll have all the love and
support you need. I promise you are loved and
cherished always.

Where's the magic?

No one ever said life would be easy, but most people are in a state of disappointment because they hoped that there would be more magic.

Hurt People

I heard hurt people, hurt people. They are only doing what comes naturally...

But what about the hurt people who don't hurt people?

The people who would hurt themselves before ever hurting another person?

It's all okay

Sometimes you'll want to hold your breath, and that's okay

Sometimes you'll want to scream underwater, and that's okay

Sometimes you'll just want to be motionless, and that's okay

..because you're not okay..but you will be.

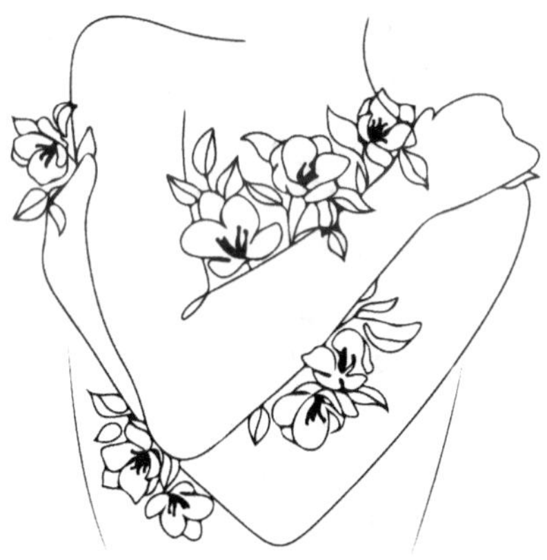

My Father's Home

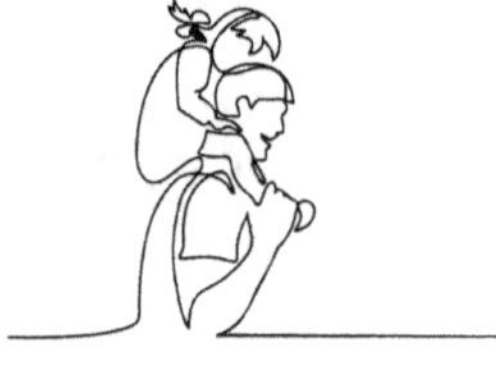

From an early age
Cooking was my father's passion.
His granny taught him how to do so.
In an appropriate fashion
She taught him how to cook Eggplant choka,
A traditional dish
How to grind turmeric and season fish.

As he got older, Arnos Vale was the spot.
Specifically, the Pizza Party Shop
After that, Argyle was the place to be.
Cookouts with friends and family

Crab, Chicken, rice, and Peas
Enjoyed under the shade of coconut trees.
Salt pan, Rawacou, Argyle, and Richmond Bay
Beaches where forever memories will stay.
Home: the intangible feeling you get in a
location, a sense of belonging, joy from loved
ones or an environment which offers tranquil
peace
Saint Vincent is my father's Home.

Fall

This season
Where I show all my forms
The colours within my soul
The cold beneath the surface
The mist in the mornings
The crisp air and silent nights
The frozen ponds, lakes and rivers
The feeling of new beginnings and final endings

H.E.L.P

You constantly search for lost souls, trying to understand them, then trying to heal them.

(H)eal and understand yourself first.

They never gave you signs, you went looking for them because you try to evaluate everyone's actions.

(E)valuate your own actions first.

They were never yours to love, but you loved them anyways.

(L)ove yourself first.

You try to persuade them, that they deserve it all. All the happiness in this world.

(P)ersuade yourself, that you are enough and you deserve every happiness in this world.
H.E.L.P Yourself First

Growing Pains

Resisting the urge to fuck it all up purpose.

Pushing to elevate your thought process.

Stop searching for satisfaction, get up and make something happen.

Let go of your ideal future and strive for an ideal mindset.

Choose to do the right thing, even if you have a habit of being self-destructive.

Not determined

The rest of your life is not determined by your experience of life so far, there's still time to change directions.

Do new things, meet new people, and walk away from any toxic connections.

Drugs

Nothing compares to forbidden love; the rush is comparable to ecstasy. The way it surrounds you then changes your body's chemistry.

The obsession is comparable to a caffeine hit, it accelerates your heart rate, and you cannot function without it.

The insecurity of it all is comparable to coming down from antidepressants, the world looks a lot scarier. Yet you still feel the brain fuzz that acts as a comforter.

I Love you.

Say 'I love you' more often.

Say it louder.

Say it with passion.

Say it with wanting.

Say it with hope.

Say it with certainty.

Say it fearlessly.

Say it now, before 'I love you too' is no longer their response.